PLATFORM PAPERS

QUARTERLY ESSAYS ON THE PERFORMING ARTS FROM CURRENCY HOUSE

No. 51
May 2017

CURRENCY HOUSE

Platform Papers Partners

Platform Papers
Readers' Forum

Readers' responses to our previous essays are posted on our website. Contributions to the conversation (250 to 2000 words) may be emailed to info@currencyhouse. org.au. The Editor welcomes opinion and criticism in the interest of healthy debate but reserves the right to monitor where necessary.

Platform Papers, quarterly essays on the performing arts, is published every February, May, August and November and is available through bookshops, by subscription and on line in paper or electronic version. For details see our website at www.currencyhouse.org.au.

MISSING IN ACTION: The ABC and Australia's screen culture

KIM DALTON

ABOUT THE AUTHOR

Kim Dalton has worked in the Australian and international film and television industry since 1973. As a practitioner and program maker he produced a number of award-winning television dramas and documentaries; and at the Australian Film Finance Corporation was involved in the financing of numerous projects. In 1992 he joined Beyond International and worked on the international financing, production and distribution of a large slate of television and feature films. From 1999, as CEO of the Australian Film Commission, Kim Dalton was responsible for overhauling its development programs, expanding its screen culture programs and ensuring the agency's and industry's engagement with digital and online technology, production and distribution. He led the policy debate around Australian content on television and was a key adviser to government on the audio-visual industries during negotiations on the Australia-US Free Trade Agreement.

As the Director of ABC TV from 2006 to 2013 he took ABC TV into the digital era, significantly expanding its broadcast and online services. He overhauled ABC TV's organisational structure and its production model, and obtained significant additional funding for increased Australian drama, documentary and children's programming.

Kim Dalton holds a Bachelor of Arts (Drama) from Flinders University of South Australia and a Postgraduate Diploma in Arts Administration from the City University of London. He is Adjunct Professor at the School of Communication and Creative Industries, University of the Sunshine Coast. In 2007 he was awarded the Order of Australia Medal for service to the film and television industry in policy, assistance to Indigenous producers and in the promotion of emerging visual technology. He has been Chair of Freeview and a board member of NIDA. He is the founding Chair of the Asian Animation Summit and a board member of Screenrights and December Media.

ACKNOWLEDGEMENTS

I owe my engagement and deep felt connection with the ABC to my father. It was a presence in my childhood—informing me, educating me, entertaining me.

I'm grateful to Katharine Brisbane and the Platform Papers editorial committee for providing me with the opportunity to write and have published this paper. For early encouragement and assistance, and then feedback and notes during the writing process, thanks to both Catriona Hughes and Max Dalton. Thanks also to a number of ex-ABC colleagues for their reflections and comments during the research phase including Tim Brooke-Hunt, Carole Sklan, Chris Oliver-Taylor and Stuart Menzies, and to Margaret Mathieson for tracking down some 'lost' documents. Thanks to Jenny Buckland for her observations and comments about the ABC and children's television and to Ian Booth for his comments about the ABC and regional production. Sandra Alexander and Nick Herd provided constructive feedback on a first draft. Ken Inglis's two volume history of the ABC was an invaluable research document. Jonathan Oldsberg's papers on the UK independent production sector and terms of trade provided useful background and insights. To my many colleagues in the independent production sector with whom I have discussed this issue, thank you.

Finally, thanks from the heart to Penny Robins, who has travelled with me for most of my career, who lived through my time at the ABC, who has lived through the long gestation of this essay and the actual wrestling of it onto paper, and who will now have to live through the robust discussion I hope it will stimulate. Without her support and advice along the way I doubt I would have made the journey.

1. INTRODUCTION

As so often is the case, timing is everything. In the late 1960s and early 70s Prime Ministers Gorton (1968–71) and Whitlam (1972–75) introduced a number of measures, including government funding and a national film and television school, with the aim of re-establishing a local film industry. In 1972 the then South Australian Premier, Don Dunstan, established the South Australian Film Corporation (SAFC) as part of a strategy for his state to participate in this revival of an Australian film industry. Experienced managers, producers and key creatives were imported from the eastern states. However, there was also a strategy in place to develop the local talent pool and to provide opportunities to local film companies and filmmakers. And in a critical policy intervention, Dunstan also gave the SAFC a budget and the sole responsibility to produce education, training and information films for all SA Government departments.

I happened to be there. In 1973, I was a final year undergraduate at Flinders University. I had left Melbourne in 1969 to attend the new drama school that had been set up by Professor Wal Cherry at Flinders. I enrolled with the ambition of training as an actor but along the way, including a year off during which I worked for a while in theatre, my interest turned to film and television.

Inevitably, I was one of the eager young hopefuls who presented at the offices of the SAFC looking for opportunities to work on its portfolio of government films. My luck was in when I was offered the role of unit manager on a series of short training films being made for the state education department. Flinders was flexible enough to allow me to take the job during my final term and have the experience count towards my degree. I graduated and went on, over the next couple of years, to work on a wide variety of government commissioned films as well as a children's television pilot, television advertisements and what became the iconic and groundbreaking Australian feature film *Picnic at Hanging Rock* (1976).

While at university and during these early years of a nascent Australian film industry my contact with the ABC was limited to driving out to the inner northern suburb of Collinswood to deliver 16mm negative for processing at Adelaide's first and only movie film laboratory. It was privately owned but conveniently situated next to the ABC's offices and studios as, in those pre electronic news-gathering days, the ABC was a major client. In the early evening or late at night after a day's filming, having pushed the film canisters into the delivery shute, I would occasionally gaze through the cyclone wire fence into the ABC compound and wonder what went on in there.

Years later—having produced drama and documentary programs for the ABC, having worked on the financing and international distribution of ABC programs, having been the Director of ABC Television for seven years and visited the Collinswood offices in that capacity on a number of occasions—that image of the ABC compound, behind a fence and a space unto itself, still resonates with me. It is an image of separation, in some respects isolation, and certainly of independence.

The opportunity I had, to embark upon and then develop a career in the Australian film and television industry, had come about as a result of a policy debate started in the 1960s. Successive Australian governments had developed and put in place a framework of regulation and funding to ensure that Australians had access to a minimum level and range of Australian programs on Australian television. A critical part of that policy framework, from the 1970s on, was the development and support of an independent production sector and a creative workforce to produce these programs; but this largely happened independently of the ABC. Policy makers and governments for the most part ignored the national broadcaster, regarding it as being quite separate and independent. And for the most part the ABC stood aside from, and at times fiercely rejected, any association or engagement with the policy debate, the evolving policy framework and, more generally, the screen production sector.

After an initial introduction to the industry in Adelaide I went on to work as an independent producer and executive producer of television dramas, documentaries and children's programs. I worked at the Australian Film Finance Corporation (FFC) contributing to the financing of feature films and television programs and observing close up the multiple stakeholder relationships and the cultural/commercial dynamic that underpins our industry. Then for five years with Beyond International, today one of Australia's largest international production companies and distributors, I gained experience in the private sector. And then, as CEO of the Australian Film Commission for six years I was able to participate in, and contribute to, the major strategic and policy debates around the development, production, distribution and broadcasting of Australian content.

In 2006 I arrived at the ABC as Director of TV and confronted for the first time the deeply entrenched and institutionalised culture of independence that exists in what is so often, and in so many ways, referred to as Australia's largest and most important cultural institution. By the time I left, some seven years later, I had achieved many things—including a significant diversion of internal resources to support increased production of Australian programs; and the largest increase ever in government funding to the ABC for Australian content. But I knew my impact on this culture had been minimal and was ultimately transitory.

This paper is an opportunity to ask how and why a cultural institution of such significance has been variously able, allowed, encouraged and supported to run its own race, to operate outside of, and with no regard for, a public policy framework for a sector of which it is a part.

2. WHAT PRICE INDEPENDENCE?

Before answering these questions and attempting to understand why the ABC is adrift in a policy sense, it is important to understand what can be achieved as a result of better practice. In this respect the last ten years provides an opportunity to observe both what happens when there is an alignment between policy settings, strategy and funding at the ABC and then what happens when the ABC decides to exercise its independence and pursue its own agenda and priorities.

The ABC received budget increases in its triennial budgets of 2006 (Howard) and 2009 (Rudd). In 2006, $10 million per annum for drama, documentary and children's content. In 2009 a staged increase in funding across the triennium would by the third year total $67 million per annum—$40 million for drama programs and $27 million for the establishment of a dedicated children's channel with a commitment to deliver 50 per cent Australian programs. All of this funding, $77 million in total, was to be ongoing beyond the triennium in which it was provided. It went into base funding and was subject to the ABC's annual indexation. The new funding represented an almost 30 per cent increase to ABC TV's budget and the impact was significant in terms of cultural and creative outcomes, industry activity and development, and the quality and quantity of Australian programs delivered to audiences.

From a base in 2006 of five hours of drama, no prime-time Indigenous content, limited Australian children's content and a limited documentary offering, within seven years ABC TV was offering Australian drama at levels approaching that of the commercial networks, a dedicated children's channel with 50 per cent of its content Australian and across all genres, and a diverse slate of Australian documentaries. For the first time on Australian television Indigenous producers, writers, directors and actors were making drama and documentary programs for prime-time slots, launching with the popular and critically acclaimed *Redfern Now* mini-series.

What is important in the context of this paper is that these outcomes were not solely the result of additional funding. Additional resources were essential; however they were provided to the ABC in support of a clearly articulated policy-based proposal and a three-pronged strategy I had developed as Director of TV, which had broad industry and public support. Firstly, the ABC committed to increased levels of Australian drama, documentary, children's and Indigenous content. Secondly, it committed to working productively and in partnership with Australia's independent production sector. Thirdly, the ABC committed to engaging strategically with federal and state funding agencies to finance its expanded slate of Australian content, including ensuring an increase in production outside Sydney and Melbourne.

In summary, the additional funding was provided in the

context of, and in support of, Australia's national screen policy framework. Over time, the Australian public and ABC TV audiences experienced this additional funding in the form of a significant increase in the volume, diversity and quality of new Australian programs appearing on their screens. The impact of this additional funding and the outcomes that flowed from it can appropriately be described as policy outcomes and these are worth some more detailed consideration across drama, children's, documentary and Indigenous work.

Drama

Looking back, we are reminded that by the mid-2000s the ABC had reduced its allocation to Australian drama to around $5 million per year. Its annual drama (and comedy) output was only twenty hours. This, of course, was far less than the Australian drama quota requirements for the commercial networks which approximates to around 90 hours per year. The Howard Government's funding in 2006 of $10 million per annum for additional Australian content provided a welcome annual budget increase to drama of $5 million. By 2009 the drama (and comedy) output had risen to 32 hours, still well short of the quota requirements for the commercial networks.

The additional funding provided to the ABC in its 2009–10 triennial funding agreement was the quantum increase required to bring the ABC's Australian drama levels up to that of the commercial networks. With funding rising over three years to ongoing and indexed funding of $40 million per year, ABC TV was able to develop a more expansive vision across telemovies, mini-series, occasional feature films, returning series and a broad slate of scripted comedy. The ABC began to work with both established independent producers and creative teams as well as relatively new entrants to television drama. It was open to a more authored approach, particularly with its shorter mini-series, and began to work with many of Australia's leading producers, writers, directors and actors.

By 2011–12 ABC TV's drama budget was close to $45 million per annum which supported a slate of almost 70 hours of drama and scripted comedy. A further six hours a year of prime-time Indigenous drama meant the ABC was within sight of reaching its stated objective to government of meeting the commercial network drama quotas. With producers able to raise money through federal and state screen agencies, including the federal Producer Offset; and bring investment into productions from international broadcasters and distributors, ABC TV's commissions were underpinning an annual drama slate in the vicinity of $100 million.

There were, of course, hits and misses as in any area of creative endeavour. However, by any measure— critical response, audience figures, local and international awards—the initiative was a success: high levels of Australian content were delivered through diverse and important stories and across a range of genres. Stories about remarkable Australians (*Mabo*), literary adaptations (*The Slap*), intelligent but off-beat comedy-drama (*Rake*) all written and produced by some of Australia's leading screen talent. For the first time, Australian producers and creative teams were able to work in the traditionally British-dominated and popular murder-mystery genre, bring an idiosyncratic Australian flavour to them and tell stories that were resonant with Australia's social history (*The Dr Blake Mysteries* and *Miss Fisher's Murder Mysteries*). Auteur comedy writers and performers created a new generation of familiar and recognisable characters, at times achingly awkward and challenging. A broad range of Australian acting talent, some new and emerging, some established, occasionally iconic, were regularly appearing on ABC TV programs.

And then, within four years of the initial announcement by the Rudd Government, the ABC decided that it had other priorities. Without announcement, consultation or discussion, from 2013–14 onwards funds were transferred out of the drama budget to other areas of the ABC. This had nothing to do with partisan politics or government budget cuts. It began to occur before the Abbott Government was elected and has continued at a level disproportionate to any cuts imposed on the ABC's budget. Only four years beyond the initial funding triennium the drama budget had been cut by somewhere in the vicinity of 20 per cent.

Children's television

The story around children's television is similarly concerning. In its triennial funding budget of 2009, the ABC received an additional and specific allocation in order to expand its children's offering. This allocation rose over three years to $27 million a year and remained at that level as part of base and indexed funding. The ABC had promised the Government and the Australian Children's Television Foundation (ACTF, its partner in a very public funding campaign) the production industry and ultimately its audiences, a dedicated channel for school-age children, with a comprehensive offering across all program genres and with an Australian content level of 50 per cent.

The pitch to government from the ABC and the ACTF was expansive. It was underpinned by the promise that the new channel would achieve 50 per cent Australian content. The Commonwealth had already been spending significant money through its screen agencies and tax-based measures on children's content to support the Children's Television Standards (CTS) drama quotas that applied to the commercial networks. As a result there was a rich legacy of work available for the new channel in the form of highly subsidised programs that had already been shown on commercial networks once or twice. The new channel would have a wide choice. It would provide a broad and comprehensive service delivering entertainment, education and information.

This was a new and very special service and the impact of this new channel was significant. The fact that the Prime Minister was invited and agreed to launch the service underlined that this was something special, that something new was being created for Australian children and their families.[1] The Australianness of the service was fundamental. It was about citizenship, about nationhood, about ensuring Australian children grew up hearing

Australian voices and Australian stories.

Within three years the ABC was delivering its 50 per cent Australian content promise on the new ABC3. Importantly, it was also delivering the diversity promised across live action drama, animation, comedy, reality, daily news and current affairs, studio-based entertainment shows and factual programs. The ABC also set out to increase the breadth and depth of the children's production sector. It did this by discovering and developing new on-screen and off-screen talent and by attracting into the children's area existing senior producers, writers and directors working in adult television. Audiences responded positively. By 2013–14 the ABC's reach among five to twelve-year-olds was 43.6 per cent and its daytime share was 30 per cent.

This initiative was transformative. Until that point the ABC's service for school-age children had been limited to morning and afternoon blocks on its main channel. Within ABC TV, and the ABC more generally, its children's offering had not been a priority and the children's budget had been steadily reduced. Ultimately, it was a service relying on cheap UK imports. The networks too were obliged under the CTS to screen some Australian children's drama but it was rarely well promoted or programmed. Neither the ABC nor the commercial networks valued children's television and argued that in any case Australian children did not want to watch it.

ABC3 went to air on 4 December 2009 and was an almost overnight success. Children found the channel quickly and as the audience figures came in the commonly held view that children did not like children's content was proved to be wrong. With funding now available, and a broad range of genres being commissioned, the Australian production industry began to take notice. Those among the larger and more established companies that had never bothered with children's television now became interested in the production and creative opportunities. Competition for commissions improved overnight, experienced creatives became involved and programs started appearing on air with levels of creative ambition and standards of writing, direction, acting and storytelling that had not until then been achieved.

However, the reality was that the ABC had never internalised the idea that children's television was important. Children's programming is just not in the DNA of the ABC. Ultimately, in the absence of commitment from individual senior managers, children's TV is not prioritised. The institutional commitment is absent and now, just a few years later, this brief period is beginning to look like a golden era that was all too soon over. Notwithstanding the very specific allocation from the Rudd Labor Government, within less than four years the ABC was reallocating these funds. While Labor was still in power up to a third of the budget had been transferred out of children's. Further cuts have been imposed in the years since: it is estimated since 2012–13 the ABC's children's budget has been reduced by 50 per cent or more than $20 million, an amount that is disproportionate to cuts the ABC received from the Abbott Coalition. The ABC also quietly halved its Australian content objective from 50 per cent to 25 per cent[2] and with fewer funds the children's department has inevitably been commissioning a less diverse slate.

Documentary

Understanding what has happened in the area of documentary at the ABC over the past ten years is more complex in terms of the issues we are exploring in this paper. The type of programming commissioned and broadcast has changed, the ABC is doing less internal production in this area, and the lines between factual and documentary have become blurred. Nonetheless, documentary programming remains an important part of the schedule. Most Australian documentary content is sourced from the independent production sector, and the relationship between the ABC and the sector remains both important and problematic.

Back in the mid-2000s, ahead of additional money being provided by the Howard Government for independently produced Australian content, the ABC had an annual documentary slate of 25 to 30 programs. This Government's first documentary initiative was to provide Film Australia with $10 million over three years to support the production of history films. The ABC provided some additional funding and partnered with Film Australia to commission these films. Soon after this initiative was in place, the ABC allocated a further $2.5m of the additional $10m of funding it had received from the Howard Government in 2006, to documentary production.

Within three years the ABC's annual independent documentary slate had doubled. With a budget of around $5.5 million the ABC Documentary Department was commissioning a slate of 55 hours and with a total production value in the vicinity of $30 million. The additional funds were coming from federal and state screen agencies, the Producer Rebate and through co-production arrangements with overseas broadcasters and international distributors. Importantly, the slate was appropriate to a public broadcaster with programs across religion, arts, natural history, science, history and contemporary social issues.

Television plays an important, arguably central, role in people's sense and understanding of their own history. History should be core to the ABC's remit. It has a responsibility to reflect our own lives back to ourselves in both a contemporary and an historical sense. By 2012–13 the ABC was commissioning and broadcasting around 15 hours of history documentaries each year. With just under $2 million of its budget allocated to history documentaries it was generating around $10 million of production. This was high value, high profile, sometimes in part dramatised and increasingly produced, written and directed by some of the Australia's most experienced factual program makers. Not all were successful, but for the most part these programs were attracting significant audiences and gaining positive critical attention.

However, once again, by 2013, the ABC had decided that documentaries in general, and history documentaries in particular, were no longer a priority. In the 2013–14 budget an estimated ten per cent of the documentary budget was re-allocated and further cuts were made in budgets that followed. By 2016 the ABC was broadcasting only one history documentary, the two-part *Howard on Menzies: Building Modern Australia*. All of this in the absence of transparency, public discussion or reference to any public policy settings.

In the area of natural history, within a few years the ABC had moved from commissioning six to eight programs a year to none. The impact on Australia's small but internationally respected natural history documentary community has been devastating, leaving them without support from a local broadcaster and forcing them to work in other genres or to operate as service providers to international broadcasters such as the BBC, whose fascination with Australia's flora and fauna remains undimmed.

Indigenous content

The ABC established an Indigenous Programs Unit in 1987. The output of the Unit was largely restricted to long-running non prime-time magazine programs with occasional short documentaries and dramas—and remained so across the next almost thirty years. Numbers of Indigenous program makers passed through the Unit, gaining valuable experience, but this was an internal production unit and its primary focus remained internal short-form magazine production, in keeping with the broader ABC's inwardly focused and very white Anglo-Saxon institutional culture. No attempt was made to establish strategic partnerships with federal and state screen agencies in support of their efforts to develop an Indigenous independent production sector nor to enable Indigenous storytelling on a larger canvas.

The development of an Indigenous production sector

therefore occurred independently of the ABC. An initial and important development in the mid-1980s was the establishment of the Central Australian Aboriginal Media Association (CAAMA) in Alice Springs. Working in both radio and video, and with support from the Australian Film Commission (AFC), CAAMA became an important centre of activity and training for young Indigenous filmmakers. Then in 1993 the AFC established its Indigenous Branch. This was the beginning of a long-term and ultimately successful strategy to deliver the training and resources necessary for Aboriginal and Torres Strait Islander people to write, direct and produce film and television programs.

The first drama initiative from the AFC's Indigenous branch in 1996 involved a partnership with SBS Independent. The initiative, titled *From Sand to Celluloid*, produced six short films from Indigenous writers and directors for broadcast on prime-time television. When I became CEO of the AFC in 1999 I inherited and continued this focused and strategic plan designed to develop an independent Indigenous screen production and creative sector with the capacity to develop, write, direct, produce and perform Indigenous stories. SBS was an important partner over a number of years in providing funds but more importantly in providing a prime-time release. For the most part, with occasional exceptions, this critical development within Australia's cultural sector was ignored by the ABC, who showed neither strategic interest nor capacity.

In 2006, on becoming Director of ABC TV, I was then in a position to include, as part of the drama funding bid to government, a commitment to develop an Indigenous independent production sector and a proposal to develop and broadcast regular Indigenous prime-time drama. An Indigenous Department was established and provided with an annual and fixed allocation from the new funding. In November 2012, following an extensive and properly funded development period, the ABC broadcast Australia's first prime-time television mini-series to be commissioned, produced, written, directed, largely performed and partly crewed by Indigenous Australians. *Redfern Now* was ground-breaking television. At its launch I said it was 'born of, is resonant of, and speaks of, Australia's Indigenous culture, its deep and profound historic roots and its vibrant and contemporary expression.'[3]

ABC TV's Indigenous Department has gone on to commission seasons of short dramas, documentaries and several feature films along with repeat and new mini-series. Although modest in terms of hours, Indigenous drama and documentary is regularly and consistently featured on ABC prime-time television and draws significant audiences along with much critical attention. A cohort of Indigenous creative talent continues to create this work while increasingly beginning to participate more widely across the broader industry.

This widely acclaimed and successful initiative has not, however, escaped the ABC's inclination to re-allocate resources away from television. In the absence of formal disclosure it is difficult to report an exact figure but it is likely that the Indigenous commissioning budget has been reduced by at least ten per cent. Less money means less development and fewer shows commissioned, or at least commissioned over a more extended period. Fewer writers are employed, fewer directors, crews and performers get to work, or work less often. Whatever the size of the reduction, it is significantly larger than the cuts imposed on the ABC by the Abbott Government and at least in part it preceded them. Ultimately, this was a decision of senior ABC management endorsed by the ABC Board to de-prioritise the commitment that had been made to the development of an Indigenous prime-time drama strand and to re-allocate the funds elsewhere within the ABC.

Regional

Finally, to the issue of the ABC's engagement with the production of drama, documentary and children's content outside Sydney and Melbourne.

The production of professional-standard and long-form screen content requires considerable infrastructure in terms of equipment, technology and a skilled workforce. Inevitably, without strategic intervention, screen industries centralise: Hollywood, London, Sydney and to a lesser extent Melbourne. Creative talent is drawn to these centres of activity. Larger production entities provide continuity of employment and security of supply to broadcasters.

However, in most countries with developed screen industries, local and state governments encourage and support the development of regional screen industries for both cultural and economic reasons. At times national policy frameworks, such as apply to the BBC in the UK, also encourage regional diversity in the production industry. Australia is no different and every state in Australia has a screen agency which with varying degrees of success has fostered local independent film sectors. What is missing in Australia is a policy framework applying to the ABC, similar to that which applies to the BBC in the UK.

The issue of the ABC's commitment to maintaining a regional presence for television production, as distinct from news gathering or local radio, has for the most part been an issue of levels of internal employment and has most often and most vocally been pursued by politicians from what ABC management refers to as the BAPH states (Brisbane, Adelaide, Perth and Hobart). In the early days of radio, and then television, the ABC operated a federated structure. For television, the technology that allows seamless and live national networking did not become available until the 1970s. Infrastructure including studios, outside broadcasting vans, production and post-production facilities along with production and technical staff were all developed and in place to generate and deliver state-based news content along with limited non-news television programs.

Regionally based teams have over the years supplied a variety of programs into the national schedule. For reasons of creative capacity, the available skills base and funds, programs have for the most part been restricted to magazine or lifestyle programs designed to be broadcast ahead of the 7.00pm news—the program that heralds the start of the ABC's prime-time schedule. However, state screen agencies aspire to a larger canvas and are interested in developing a local creative sector that can produce long-form programming that will screen both nationally and on occasions internationally. And while the ABC, the national broadcaster, should be a natural partner in encouraging and supporting a diversity of voices and creativity, partnerships in this area have been difficult to sustain. Western Australia provides an interesting case history.

ScreenWest

In 2005 the West Australian Government's screen agency, ScreenWest, established a Matched Prime Time Fund. The fund essentially was a sum of money set aside to encourage and to assist the ABC to work with the local production community to produce programs out of WA for the prime-time schedule. After a slow start and few outcomes, in the context of the ABC's increasing high-end documentary slate, the ABC agreed to focus on working with WA's small but established factual production companies.

Over a period of a few years, WA's factual production sector moved from single project-based companies producing one-off natural history or observational documentaries to high-end high-budget docu-dramas, often co-produced with international broadcasters and attracting large national audiences when screened on the ABC. This increase in production activity led to the development of a broad skills set resident in WA, including editing and production design. It was also aligned with a growth in the feature industry.

Before this joint initiative began the ABC was spending just over $1 million annually on productions commissioned from WA companies with total budgets amounting to around $4 million. As a result of the initiative and active engagement from the ABC, in 2012–13 the ABC spent $8 million on WA productions and in total their budgets amounted to $20 million. This was a significant injection into the WA independent screen sector which resulted in an increase in levels of employment and in the skills and depth of crews in WA. Importantly, it also allowed a number of WA independent production companies to consolidate their operations, to retain a full-time staff and to develop a much needed research and development capacity.

In parallel with this initiative, ScreenWest and the ABC had also identified a lack of skills and experience in WA in the area of shorter run and lower budget factual series. A capacity-building joint initiative was instigated involving development funding and a commitment from the ABC to commission multiple series. Ultimately five series were commissioned and screened nationally, one of which, *Who's Been Sleeping in My House?*, became an established format and was re-commissioned a number of times. A strategic response from the ABC, a partnership with a regional screen agency, increased regional content and improved infrastructure and skills base across a number of production companies.

And then, a change of direction from the ABC and a withdrawal from these regional commitments. Again in the absence of any consultation or consideration of the impact on a local production sector. By 2014–15 the ABC had reduced its spend with WA production companies to less than $0.1 million.

When the national broadcaster withdraws almost $8 million of expenditure in the space of two years, the impact on a relatively small regional industry is dramatic. Production companies downsize, creative talent and crew move interstate, overseas broadcasters and distributors look elsewhere for partnerships. Years of investment in talent and skill is discarded.

Policy, strategy and outcomes

The purpose of setting out this brief history of funding, commissioning activity and program outcomes over the past ten years is not to re-live some glorious moments or lay a claim to past successes. Rather, it is to demonstrate that a combination of coherent public policy, adequate funding and strategic engagement by the ABC can deliver positive results for ABC audiences, including to children, Australia's cultural output, the independent production sector and the creative sector more generally.

In the period 2006 through to 2013 a significant and targeted increase in government funding was available to the ABC. The ABC used this funding in a highly strategic manner and the outcomes were by any measure impressive.

The strategic settings and behaviour of the ABC were instigated and driven by myself and my executive management team, a group of strategically motivated people with an understanding of and commitment to public broadcasting, a depth of experience in the creation of television content and strong links to the independent production sector. We also brought a background in policy formulation and of working in public sector environments where transparency is mandatory. What has become clear in the last few years is that this was a passing moment in the history of the ABC. The competencies and the commitment that this particular executive group brought to the ABC were not those of the institution itself. More importantly, there are no governance and accountability structures in place to sustain the alignment between public policy and ABC strategy.

The erosion begins

And so the ABC re-allocates and reduces funds provided to it by government exclusively for Australian adult and children's content, for the development of a strong Indigenous voice, for the documenting of our history and natural history, and for regional diversity.

The lag time for the on-screen impact of decisions like this is often two to three years. The impact on the production industry is more immediate. While larger production companies can trim their operations and look elsewhere for work, the impact on individual writers, crews and performers, particularly in the area of children's TV and in some regional areas, has been significant.

All of this occurs largely in a cone of silence, created by the ABC but accepted by government and effectively endorsed by many of its supporters. The ABC ultimately is not called to account over publicly taking money from government on the promise of 50 per cent Australian content on its children's channel, only to privately decide that 25 per cent is enough. The ABC can bask in positive reviews for *Redfern Now* only to quietly shift money away from Indigenous drama a few years later. Audiences flock to the ABC to watch stories of some iconic events and characters in Australian history, or to discover the wonders of our flora and fauna, but when nothing is offered they have no choice but to watch another UK import. There is little or no consistency or transparency around the reporting of any of this. *Furthermore, the Government has no mechanism whereby it monitors or establishes requirements for the ABC's performance in regard to its Australian content or its engagement with the independent production sector.* To do so would immediately lead to a chorus of claims about infringement of the ABC's independence.

In the following two sections of this paper I will explore how a situation has evolved whereby the ABC is able to put its own agenda and priorities ahead of national policy settings. To understand how the ABC is able to position itself we need to go back to the introduction of television into Australia.

3. AUSTRALIAN TELEVISION CONTENT AND A PUBLIC POLICY FRAMEWORK

Television arrived in Australia in 1956, initially as a series of trial broadcasts in Sydney on the commercial broadcaster TCN9 and soon after in Melbourne. In designing and outlining a plan for television services the Menzies Government had committed to a dual public and private system of ownership, similar to that which existed in radio. Accordingly, the ABC began broadcasting in Melbourne and Sydney in November of that year in time for the Melbourne Olympics. By 1960 the ABC and two commercial operators were broadcasting in all capital cities; by 1962 television had arrived in Canberra and a growing number of regional centres across the country.

Australian content on this new medium was an issue even before the first television broadcasts began. The power of television and its impact culturally was immediately recognised. For some, it was a matter of concern. In 1952, Prime Minister Menzies, had been reported as saying: 'I hope this thing will not come to Australia within my term of office.'[4] About that he was wrong. The economics of television had also been quickly understood, especially the figures that showed that foreign programs could be purchased at a fraction of the cost of local production.

The Royal Commission on Television in 1954 established by the Menzies Government became the birthing place for what would become the long-running public policy debate around Australian screen content. The Commission recommended the dual public and private system of ownership; and while it ultimately did not find in favour of proposals put forward for strict local content quotas, it did nonetheless stress the importance of local content on this new medium. As important, though, for the purposes of this paper, was its statement that broadcasters had 'an obligation, [...] to ensure that the best use was made of Australian talent'.[5] This sentiment was reinforced by the Minister when speaking to the Broadcasting and Television Bill 1956: 'The Government expects stations to afford the maximum practicable amount of employment for Australians in the production and presentation of programs.'[6]

In the early days of television, issues of program supply and the capacity of the local industry to produce quality content were common to the commercial broadcasters and the ABC. Unlike the UK and the US, Australia had no local feature film industry which could supply existing and new content to the emerging medium. Furthermore the technology of early television required a substantial investment in infrastructure as so much of it was live and studio based. Television required substantial infrastructure and was labour intensive; and as a result broadcasters were producers of content as much as they were distributors of content. In short, television required an institutional solution— at least at this early stage.

In 1956 the ABC was already a large organisation with a staff of around 1,800 producing and distributing radio programs across the country.[7] It was a natural, albeit technically and creatively challenging, extension to its operations to produce and deliver a television service. Furthermore, there was no reason to find a different industrial model, especially one that would involve the supply of programs from a virtually non-existent independent production sector. In his book *Networking: Commercial Television in Australia* Nick Herd notes:

> *This form of cultural production [external production], one nominally independent from, but structurally related to, the broadcasters, seems familiar now, but it was relatively rare in the development of most television systems until the 1980s.*[8]

Herd charts the discourse and the various interventions around Australian content on commercial television since its inception. According to Herd, 'the turbulent history of Australian content regulation is probably the most traversed area of commercial television's history.'[9] As early as 1959 we see Hector Crawford, owner of the successful independent radio drama production house and actively attempting to expand into television production, begin a campaign around the issue of Australian content, critical of what he considered to be very low levels, stating that, 'what local material there was seemed to be cheaply produced with little cultural merit'.[10]

The rise of the content quota

The first Australian content quota was introduced in 1960. It became a minimum requirement that 40 per cent of programs transmitted in prime-time by the commercial broadcasters be Australian. This rose to 45 per cent in 1962. By this stage 'the lines of debate over the Australian content issue were drawn up'.[11] The cause, and the impetus, was cultural nationalism but the context and the opposing forces were industrial and commercial. On one side were the unions and guilds representing the cultural and creative workforce, alongside a small number of independent producers such as Hector Crawford; and on the other the broadcasters who were primarily concerned about the additional cost of increased levels of Australian content.

In response to the growing level of debate the Government established a Senate Select Committee chaired by Senator Seddon Vincent. Its report, which, according to Herd, was largely ignored, nonetheless set out in strong terms the important cultural influence of television and the case for higher levels of Australian content. Understanding the essentially industrial nature of this debate, in which the only other contributors saw television as trivial or harmful, is important in understanding the relationship the ABC has since had and continues to have with this debate.

Herd provides a useful summary of the four groups who presented to the Committee:

> *the broadcasters, mainly concerned with highlighting the difficulties of finding resources and talent [...]; the cultural workers wanting to refute this and to advance proposals for government intervention that would improve their employment prospects; the educationists eager to prove the triviality of television and its deleterious effect on the young; and religious groups worried about the effect of television on public morals. Thus we have two essentially industrial groups engaged in a dialogue about the material conditions of cultural production, and two groups representing those who had been fearful of the introduction of television in the first place, now wishing to make known that their fears had been largely realised.[12]*

This debate continues, with various content levels and quota milestones and beachheads being established along the way. In the fracturing digital environment Australian content has become such a critical component and point of difference in the commercial free-to-air offering that the commercial broadcasters are for the most part more accepting of this aspect of the regulatory environment. Australian content is now the most popular content on Australian television: it attracts the increasingly elusive large aggregated audiences and it underpins the business model. Its popularity with audiences and its economic importance to the Australian production industry are now important factors in the political dynamics of our licence and regulatory system, including the maintenance of Australia's strong sport anti-siphoning regime.[13]

The growth of the independent production sector and the relationship between its health and resilience and that of the broader cultural and creative sector becomes increasingly part of the debate and the policy framework. In the 1970s, we see 'the development of drama as being linked to the development of theatre and features in Australia [...W]ithout healthy activity in all these sectors the pool of creative resources available to television would be weak.'[14] In the 1980s we see continuing strong representation of the argument that a consistent supply of quality Australian content to meet regulatory requirements requires a strong independent production sector and that broadcasters must play a role 'in ensuring the security and the development of the sector in the future'.[15]

By the 1980s, the industry was also promoting the view that television was an important part of Australia's cultural output, that the work of the television industry had lasting cultural value and, importantly, that it was 'the major outlet for our media arts'.[16] This view was supported by the cultural economists David Throsby and Greg Withers, in a report to the Australia Council: 'There is evident a real lack of understanding on the part of both the traditional arts and the newer media of their complementarity'.[17]

From that time government policy formulation around Australian screen content has been informed by the view that a sustainable and vibrant independent production industry was a fundamental tenet of the policy framework.

Agencies were established—initially the Australian Film Commission, then the Film Finance Corporation and now Screen Australia—to support and develop the industry. Tax incentives were adopted and then abandoned in the 1980s in favour of direct funding, then re-introduced in a new form in 2007. Definitions of Australian content have eschewed any on-screen test and go instead to the Australian origin of the script, the Australian ownership of copyright, the employment of Australians in key creative roles and budgets spent on Australian elements. Screen Australia television funding is only available to companies independent of broadcasters. The taxation measures now in place to support television drama and documentary programs are in part designed to assist the sustainability of independent production companies, although they also benefit commercial broadcasters who produce their own drama and documentary.

In summary, this public policy framework has been developed to support and sustain Australia's cultural output and the capacity to produce it. The cultural purpose and intentions of the framework are well established and explicitly stated in the findings of reviews and Ministerial statements and commitments, as well as in the rationales supporting content regulations and taxation measures, and in the objectives and work of funding agencies. The Australian Government's peak broadcasting regulatory body, the Australian Communications and Media Authority (ACMA), encapsulates this fundamental policy intention in articulating as one of its objectives the promotion of 'the role of broadcasting in developing and reflecting a sense of Australian identity character and cultural diversity'.[18]

4. WHOSE ABC?

So, if over a period of more than sixty years Australia has steadily developed a public policy framework that strategically connects Australian screen content and the screen industry and creative sector that produces it, where does the ABC fit within or align with this framework? After all, the ABC is a broadcaster and, as for other broadcasters, we should be concerned about the cultural significance and influence of its output. It operates in a common environment and the same conditions apply as for other broadcasters where low-cost foreign programming is privileged economically over more expensive local programming. And like other broadcasters the ABC has the potential to contribute to the wellbeing or otherwise of the independent production industry and creative sector.

In addition to its existence as a broadcaster, the ABC is itself a cultural institution. This is the core and defining description regularly applied to the ABC. A description that transcends politics. Paul Keating described the ABC as 'Australia's pre-eminent cultural organisation',[19] and Richard Alston referred to it as a 'vital national cultural institution.'[20] John Howard described the ABC as a 'builder of national identity'.[21] ABC Chair 1996–2006, Donald McDonald, believed the ABC to be 'one of Australia's greatest cultural institutions'[22] and the ABC's outgoing Chair, James Spigelman, has stated that the ABC, 'throughout its 80-year history, has been, and remains, one of the most important cultural institutions in this nation.'[23] Beyond the political sphere, arts journalist and social commentator Ben Eltham, in his 2016 Platform Paper described the ABC as 'arguably the single most important cultural institution of the Australian nation-state'.[24]

All of which begs the question: where is Australia's national broadcaster and major cultural institution positioned in relation to Australia's well established Australian screen content, broadcasting and production industry and creative sector public policy framework? The answer, unfortunately, is that it operates outside of this framework in terms of formal governance arrangements, its own policies and strategies, and all too often in terms of its practice. The ABC, as Eltham writes, 'pursues its own turbulent existence as a quasi-independent body'.[25]

What is challenging about the ABC's independence from the nation's broadcasting and production sector policy framework is that the issue itself is not on anyone's agenda. Certainly not the ABC's, but also neither that of either major political party, nor the supporters of the ABC such as the Friends of the ABC (FABC) and not even the media or cultural commentariat. The only group consistently to pursue this issue is, as could be expected, the production industry and creative sector; and they are judged by almost all the previous groups as being tainted by private enterprise and motivated by self-interest.

The primary concern of the ABC is to protect its institutional status and structure and it has largely been successful in establishing and maintaining a no-go area behind a defensive barrier built on an all-encompassing notion of 'independence'. Not just editorial independence, but independence in every respect, including from national policy settings in the areas of broadcasting, Australian content and Australia's production and creative sector.

In order to challenge the ABC's independence, which it regards as immutable and unquestionable, we need to look separately at three overlapping areas: governance, the policy platforms and positions of the two major political parties; and the ABC's approach to the principles of accountability and transparency.

Governance

The ABC is established as an independent statutory authority and the government of the day has limited capacity to directly influence its policies or its operations. Nonetheless, the ABC has a public purpose, it is an instrument of government charged with certain functions and funded, adequately or inadequately, to deliver on those functions. What has become unclear over the years is the scope and clarity of the ABC's public purpose: its functions, and the allocation of its resources. This is all contested territory as is appropriate in a robust democracy. However, the discourse has become too narrow: broader and more important policy issues have been excluded.

The ABC's public purpose in broad terms is spelt out in its Charter, a creation of the 1983 Act. K.S. Inglis describes the Charter as a 'novelty',[26] an invention of an anonymous public servant of the time. The functions set out in the Charter could have been, as is usually the case, just another set of clauses in the Act. However, as Inglis wryly observes, the heading of Charter within the Act 'set[s] the list of ABC functions in a frame and dignif[ied] it with a name that rang out like the chimes of Big Ben. Soon champions of the ABC would invoke the charter as if meddling or mean politicians were King Johns aspiring to violate a broadcasting Magna Carta.'[27]

The Charter provides a legislative base to the ABC's responsibilities with regard to an Australian national identity and the cultural diversity of its community. Beyond this it is required to entertain, inform and provide 'programs of an educational nature'. The only guidance in regard to Australia's cultural output and its creative community is the requirement that it should 'encourage and promote the musical, dramatic and other performing arts in Australia'.[28] Arguably a very narrow, somewhat old-fashioned, and potentially elitist, instruction that ignores whole areas of contemporary creative practice including screen production.

Beyond the Charter though, there is no indication from government of just what the ABC is meant to do, how it is meant to do it or to what end. The reality is that when it comes to the ABC's commitment to or engagement with Australian screen content in its many forms, not only is there no framework or guidance, there simply is no mention.

Peter Lewis in his 2014 review of the ABC commented that the Corporation *may justify everything from production of Australian drama and major news gathering resources, through to broadcasting of a local sporting competition in a state or region as being consistent with Charter obligations.*[29]

Perhaps Lewis made this comment in reference to a motion moved by Greens Senator Sarah Hanson-Young, on behalf of a cross-party group (Greens, Labor Party, Liberal Party and Senator Nick Xenophon) of South Australian senators, which urged the ABC to continue its coverage of local Australian-rules football matches on the grounds that it was 'consistent with the ABC's charter [to] contribute to national identity and cultural diversity'.[30]

The ABC itself is able to reference the Charter in the most general of terms to create its own self-referential virtuous circle that lacks any transparency; such as its 2013–16 Strategic Plan: 'We are delivering on our Charter obligations. Our programming contains content of wide appeal and specialist interest […] We have a commitment to telling Australian stories.'[31]

Which, of course, can be regarded as corporate reporting speak but importantly goes to the fact that 'The Charter [itself] offers little direct guidance as [it is a] broad statement of Parliamentary intent.'[32] Lewis goes on to make the point that in the absence of an 'additional mechanism' the ABC operates with a lack of transparency around the setting of priorities and the allocation of resources.

This is not to say that since the inception of ABC television, the level and nature of Australian content has not been an ongoing issue. It has—within the organisation itself, within the industry and creative sector and in the broader community. However, the parameters of that discussion have been mostly confined to the role and expectations of the ABC as a public broadcaster; and again referenced back to the Charter. Quantity and quality are discussed, debated and assessed solely against what may or may not be good public broadcasting practice or statements drawn from the Charter. Politicians, journalists and commentators and the FABC all agree on a regular basis that as a public broadcaster the ABC should prioritise Australian content; should have a commitment to Australian stories and Australian drama; should show quality programs; and so on. However, what any of this means in practice, how it should be measured or assessed, how the ABC should be held to account, is rarely addressed.

The ABC itself makes broad and sweeping statements about its intentions and its commitments. In 2015, 'The ABC's vision is to be the independent home of Australian conversations, culture, and stories'.[33] In 2016 'The ABC provides audiences with access to extraordinary Australian content.'[34] These statements were made in the context of a ten per cent reduction in the hours of local drama and comedy screened during these years (65 and 58 hours respectively). Ten years previously, in 2005, the first objective of the ABC's Corporate Plan was to 'Contribute to a sense of national identity' and in pursuit of this, 'ABC Television broadcast distinctive content [and] the service reflected and described the Australian experience.'[35] These statements are made in the context of the 'tiny figure'[36] of five hours of drama screened that year.

The Dix Report

The modern ABC was established as a result of the Australian Broadcasting Corporation Act 1983. This Act was the central recommendation of the Fraser Government's Dix Report, tabled in Parliament in 1981. The Act established the ABC's governance structure but also its oft referred to Charter.

The Dix Report 'was received in Parliament with non-partisan respect'.[37] However, a year later, there had been no response from the Government. According to Inglis this delay was in part because the then Minister, Neil Brown, found dealing with the ABC challenging. Inglis quotes Brown as saying that the ABC 'jealously guarded [its] independence and resented any intrusion by [government]', and 'went into paroxysms of rage if a minister sought to intervene in any of their activities'. This was 'political interference, to be resisted at every turn'.[38] Actual, perceived and alleged political interference is a theme running through Inglis's forensic two-volume history of the ABC, in regard to politically sensitive issues in particular programs, coverage of contentious or contested issues, the ABC's industrial relations and management practices, certain high-profile program makers, producers or presenters, and the expansion or curtailing of services. Over the years 'political interference' has taken the form of public commentary and criticism from Prime Ministers through to individual politicians, private exchanges between Ministers and ABC chairs and managing directors, as well as, of course, the calling of independent and parliamentary reviews and the appointment of commissioners and board directors of particular political persuasions.

There is no doubt that political interference has been attempted by all sides of politics, at times successfully. At other times it has been fended off by brave chairs and managing directors or by bureaucratic dissembling and institutional circling of the wagons. Sometimes public outrage, campaigns and pressure have come to the fore to defend the ABC or to pressure it. The ABC itself and so much about it, including what and how it does it, is contested territory.

However, what is undeniable, and what has been in place since its establishment and then re-enforced in 1983, is the ABC's structural separation and independence from government. The ABC is a statutory authority, a form of governance whereby 'governments set limits to their own authority'.[39] Ultimately the ABC operates at arm's length, albeit through a Board appointed by Government. Importantly, also, the Managing Director is appointed by the Board, not by the Government. While this structure ensures independence, it poses challenges around the relationship between the ABC and broader areas of public policy. Editorial independence is fundamental to public broadcasting. However, the principle of the ABC's independence has become a mechanism for the ABC to avoid scrutiny and accountability and to avoid engagement with important areas of public policy.

Neither major political party has been prepared to tackle the issue of the ABC's governance and distinguish between its editorial independence and the independence from public policy that over time it has claimed for itself.

Accordingly, neither Party has developed a consistent and coherent policy framework in relation to Australian content on the ABC or the ABC's relationship to the independent production sector. This has been exacerbated by the fact that both major political parties have a history when in government of making appointments to the ABC Board that are largely political in nature—a habit which has led to the absence of specialist knowledge of broadcasting and the production of screen content. The Board then appoints the managing director. In sharp contrast to the BBC, which with rare exception has appointed its director general from a television background, the ABC has never had a managing director with any background or experience in screen content or its creation.

Liberal Party policy

A review of Liberal Party policy documents from the 2007, 2010, 2013 and 2016 elections reveals that the only policy document that specifically references the ABC is that which supported John Howard's November 2007 election commitment to fund the ABC to establish a dedicated children's channel.[40] The document pledges $82 million over four years to establish the new digital channel, and outlines the Coalition's policies for digital transition and the expansion of radio services. But the focus of the announcement was the children's channel initiative and there was no reference to the level of Australian content or the independent production industry.[41]

During this period the only other intervention by the

Howard Government was a funding initiative in 2006 designed to increase levels of Australian content commissioned from independent producers. An additional $10 million per annum was allocated specifically for that purpose.[42] ABC TV responded with published guidelines outlining the allocation of the funding across documentary, adult and children's drama and committing to a commissioning process that would ensure 100 per cent of this funding would go to independently produced programs.

My point here is that neither of these initiatives, welcome though they were at the time, were policy interventions. Notwithstanding the FABC's objections to tied funding, the proposal came with the barest of indications about the Government's intentions. They wanted a dedicated children's channel and they wanted additional content to be produced by the independent production sector. Howard lost the November 2007 election, the children's channel funding never eventuated and it was left to the ABC to develop a framework for allocating and spending the additional independent content funding. With the passing of the triennium these funds became part of the ABC's base funding to be allocated as it chose. It was a policy moment at best, with no assured or secured long-term impact or outcome.

Although formal Liberal Party policy in regard to the ABC may be limited, it is worth noting that the Mansfield Report was commissioned by the Howard Government.[43] Beyond being positive about the ABC and the importance of its role in Australia's broadcasting system, it provided considered and still relevant views on how to encourage the ABC to work more closely with the independent production sector.

Labor Party policy

Over the past ten years Labor Party policy around the ABC has been more extensive but has lacked consistency. While in office it has failed to develop and put in place mechanisms to achieve policy objectives and delivery over the long term.

The Labor Party 2007 National Conference—as part of its Arts, Culture and Heritage policy—outlined a number of high-level commitments to supporting and financing the film and television industry, maintaining local content requirements in the broadcasting sector and supporting high levels of local content on the ABC. However, ahead of the November 2007 election Peter Garrett, Shadow Minister for the Arts, released a more specific set of ALP policy initiatives. Under the heading, 'Building a Sustainable Film and Television Industry' Garrett's 'New Directions for the Arts' election manifesto described the ABC as a 'platform for local creativity' and committed to adequate funding to ensure the ABC could deliver 'substantial levels of Australian content'.[44] It also committed to amending the ABC Charter 'to mandate minimum levels of Australian drama [...] reflecting the similar obligations that apply to commercial television networks'.

This was a major policy initiative and broke new ground. Importantly, it had its origins in an industrial base through the Media, Entertainment and Arts Alliance (MEAA), the union representing Australia's creative professionals and in particular Australia's actors and film and television freelance technicians. The policy proposed regulating the ABC to deliver Australian content, to serve as a platform for Australia's creative talent and to contribute towards a sustainable film and television industry. For the first time in the ABC's history and in the history of Australian broadcasting policy development, the functions and role of the ABC were aligned within the ALP's platform and election manifesto and associated with the cultural imperative around Australian screen content and the industry and creative sector that produced it.

The ALP won the election and the funding to meet the drama commitment was substantially provided by the Rudd Government in its second budget along with funding to establish a dedicated children's channel with 50 per cent Australian content. On budget night 2009 Communications Minister Senator Stephen Conroy was able to announce that 'additional funding will allow the ABC to provide similar levels of Australian drama as that required of the commercial broadcasters' along with funding for a 'new digital-only children's channel [that] will provide a high level of age-appropriate, Australian entertainment and educational material.'[45] A staged increase in funding would within three years provide the ABC with an additional $40 million a year for drama production on an ongoing and indexed basis; and $27 million a year ongoing and indexed for its children's channel. The 2009 budget provided the ABC with 'the largest funding increase since its incorporation in 1983'.[46]

Of course, the additional funding provided to the ABC was not just an outcome of good policy. A wide range of individuals and organisations had worked long and hard to persuade the Government to put the policy into practice. The production industry came together and presented a united voice to the Government. The ACTF lobbied extensively. FABC, notwithstanding its dislike of tied funding, supported the bid. And as Director of ABC TV at the time, I devoted almost as much time to getting support internally for the funding bid, briefing politicians, the industry and the media, as I did to my day job and running the network.

The policy framework was critical. It supported the bid and ultimately provided the rationale for the Government's decision. A decade later in the absence of that framework, the ABC has returned to business as usual. There has been a re-allocation of resources away from Australian content alongside a souring of its relationship with the independent production sector.

What might have been

It is important as part of this story to understand that the 2007 Labor Party platform and Garrett's election manifesto were high points in the area of policy we are discussing. However, the alignment of policy objectives around Australian content, the ABC, the production industry and creative sector was all too short.

Firstly, and perhaps most importantly, the Rudd Government did not follow through on its commitment to make minimum levels of Australian drama on the ABC a Charter requirement. The ABC successfully opposed the move on the grounds that it would represent an intrusion on the ABC's independence. Notwithstanding the ABC's track record over the years of not prioritising the allocation of resources to Australian content in general and Australian drama and children's content in particular, the argument has continued to be put that it must not be given directions in regard to its programming. The solution has always been adequate funding, not specific Charter requirements.

Then in 2009 the ALP's national platform dropped any reference to the ABC, including its commitment to match local content requirements, and reduced the broadcasting and film and television policy to the reprise of a single paragraph. A sharp reverse from the 2007 platform, that committed high-level support and finance to the film and television industry and maintained local content requirements on free-to-air (commercial) and pay television. The 2011 national platform (under Prime Minister Julia Gillard) travelled further down this path and dropped all reference to broadcasting, media, the ABC, SBS, film and television and Australian content.

In March 2013 the then Minister for the Arts, Simon Crean, released a major arts policy document, *Creative Australia: National Cultural Policy*,[47] the successor to *Creative Nation* delivered by Paul Keating in 1994. Crean resigned soon after; but *Creative Australia* remained as the ALP's core policy document through to the next election. In it a number of initiatives were outlined for the screen industries, including a commitment to extend local content quotas to the commercial networks' new digital channels. The ABC, alongside the Australia Council, Screen Australia and SBS, is described as a major 'cultural organisation'[48] and these organisations are charged with being 'the principal stewards of Australian cultural heritage and its contemporary manifestations'. Significantly, *Creative Australia* confirms the clear policy link between the production of Australian screen content and a production sector with the capacity to produce it—'[e]nsuring we have an innovative and sustainable local production industry in the future is a priority'.[49] Later in the document it reiterates this position with: 'What will persist over the next ten years is an expectation and desire for Australian content to be available [...] and for Australia to have a dynamic creative sector to provide that content.'[50] Then, most importantly, from the point of this paper, the ABC's additional drama funding, an outcome of the Labor Party's 2007 policy and election platform, is listed as one of a number of initiatives designed to 'lay the foundations for the launch of a national cultural policy'.[51]

As I have outlined previously, the reality is that while the Government may have thought it had provided funds and had a plan in place whereby the ABC was a part of its policy on Australian screen content and a vibrant local production sector, the then Managing Director of the ABC, Mark Scott, the ABC Chairman, Jim Spigelman, and the ABC Board, clearly had a different view. Within four months of Prime Minister Gillard's launch of this major policy document the ABC was re-allocating funds away from Australian content generally, and away from adult drama, children's programs, documentary and

Indigenous programs in particular.

It is difficult to understand why, in 2007, there was a peak in Labor Party broadcasting and production industry policy scope and commitment, which was followed in 2009 by an increase in funding to support that policy; but which by 2011 was completely absent. Perhaps it was felt that the job had been done, the policy settings and funding set in place and they could move on. In 2013 *Creative Australia* reiterated some of these earlier elements and included the ABC in a broad policy statement around broadcasting, Australian content and the production industry. Meanwhile down the road the ABC was clearly not paying attention to any of it but pursuing its own agenda.

Transparency and Accountability

An analysis of the type being undertaken here is inevitably made difficult by the lack of transparency and accountability around ABC funding and outputs. It is easy to make announcements, as politicians like to do around important initiatives, but ensuring longer-term reporting on these initiatives is more of a challenge. And once again, the ABC can stand behind its 'independence' in the face of calls for greater transparency.

The ABC acknowledged in part the additional funding in its Annual Report for 2008–09: 'In the 2009–10 Federal Budget, $67 million was allocated to a dedicated children's channel, ABC3.'[52] In fact this statement was quite misleading, possibly consciously so, as the funding in fact was $27 million per year indexed and ongoing. There is no specific reference to the actual amount of increased funding for drama. Furthermore, there is no record in the report of the commitments made to government, to the production industry, to the ACTF, to the FABC and to others who made representations to the Government in support of this additional funding. These included a commitment to 50 per cent Australian content on the new children's channel and levels of Australian drama similar to that of the commercial networks.

By 2011–12, the final year of the triennium, and then for the first year of the next triennium, the ABC was allocating almost $40 million for its children's services and close to $50 million for its drama output. Come the 2013–14 budget, however, the ABC began to re-allocate these funds according to its own internal priorities—with no announcement, no consultation with the production industry or other stakeholders such as the ACTF, no reporting of its decision in its annual reports and no information provided about where the money had gone. What has followed over time has been a steady reduction in levels of commissioning from the ABC, levels of production and related employment in the independent sector, and a reduction in Australian content levels in areas of both children's content and drama.

This reallocation had started in 2013, well ahead of the budget cuts imposed by the Abbott Government. Furthermore, the cuts introduced by the Abbott Government, initially in May 2014, then November 2014, amounted to an overall reduction in the ABC's budget in the region of $50 million a year or approximately five per cent per annum. Under the cloak of these cuts the ABC was then able to reduce children's funding by an estimated 50 per cent and drama funding by 25 per cent. Other areas, including documentary and Indigenous drama, were also cut by disproportionate levels. In total, somewhere in the vicinity of $40 million was removed from ABC TV's budget in the following three years and re-allocated elsewhere within the Corporation. This represented a reduction of around 17 per cent, a significant amount of which had been provided to the ABC to support a major policy initiative in Australian content, the production industry and the creative sector. All this was able to be done in the name of independence and in the absence of any public scrutiny.

It is important for me at this point to state that I believe the ABC is underfunded. Furthermore, I think it unfortunate that the funding cuts introduced by Malcolm Turnbull as the ABC's Minister in the Abbott Government, were made in the absence of a firm commitment from the ABC in regard to its levels of expenditure on Australian content.

Turnbull took the view that these savings, totalling $254 million over five years, would not and should not impact programming. In a speech announcing the budget cuts he stated:

> *The savings announced today are not of a scale that requires any particular change to programming. All of the savings can be found within operational efficiencies of the kind canvassed in the Lewis Efficiency Study.*[53]

The ABC quickly signalled that this would not be the case: notwithstanding the Minister's assurances about quarantining programming from the cuts, how the ABC dealt with this reduction in funding was entirely a matter for the ABC. The Managing Director Mark Scott played the independence card immediately, responding:

> *Decisions regarding how the funding is allocated, the shape of the services the ABC delivers, and how the ABC is managed and organised, rest with the independent ABC Board.*

Ultimately, the funding argument around the ABC is political in nature, circular and without reference points. What does 'adequate' funding mean when all anyone can point to is its Charter? The Charter which can be regarded as an important foundation but which nonetheless is no more than a list of high level intentions based on a view of public broadcasting, public good and public purpose that in 1983 had had bi-partisan political, and broad community, support. And even then without reference to broader policy considerations.

The ABC and the public interest

However, the joker in the pack, the trump card, is always in the hand of the ABC. Not with Parliament, the Minister, stakeholders such as the production industry, the ACTF, or the FABC, and certainly not the broader public. In every debate, in every discussion about the

ABC's services, its operations, its allocation of resources, where it should sit or where it positions itself in broader policy frameworks such as Australian drama, children's television or Australia's creative community, finally the ABC draws the line, brings down the shutters, circles the wagons, and claims its independence. It can propose a children's channel, support the proposal by promising high levels of Australian content and be funded to do it—and then some four years later decide that it has alternative priorities and shift more than 50 per cent of that funding elsewhere—that is independence. It can decide to engage with Screen Australia and a nascent Indigenous production sector to develop and produce prime-time drama and documentaries and achieve additional funding to do so, and then decide to reduce that funding disproportionate to any funding cut it may have received—then that is independence.

Few would disagree that the ABC's editorial independence must be preserved, protected and where necessary vigorously defended. It is what distinguishes a public broadcaster from a state broadcaster. However, the ABC is also a public institution established by Parliament and funded by the taxpayer. It is Australia's major cultural institution and the public interest in its services and its operations rightfully extend to its engagement with, and its impact on, the country's cultural output and its creative capacity. As I have argued above, aligned and integrated policy frameworks are in place to support and develop Australia's cultural practice and the creation of Australian work, including its film and television industry. The ABC's independence should not extend to it standing outside and failing to actively engage with these frameworks. Nor should governments on the one hand support and develop these policy frameworks for one part of the cultural sector while allowing what is generally agreed to be Australia's major cultural institution to operate outside them.

5. An ABC of unfair trade

Earlier in this paper I outlined the impact in cultural, creative and program terms of an alignment between policy settings, adequate funding and a strategic partnership between the ABC and the independent production sector. However, a number of obstacles stand in the way of an equal and productive partnership. Some of these are structural and they exist in all broadcasting systems.

The ABC is not given to partnerships. At a management level the culture of independence has the primary focus of preserving and maintaining its institutional base and extends to how it conducts its business and commercial relationships with independent producers. The ABC, particularly in its corporate areas, is largely staffed by people whose experience is restricted to the ABC itself, or the public sector more generally. There is also an ideologically based and politically motivated mistrust of independent producers, at times amounting to outright opposition. This is driven by the Commonwealth Public Service Union (CPSU) on the grounds that these producers are primarily motivated by commercial gain.[54] In this the ABC always has the cooperation of the leadership of the FABC[55] and an array of politicians particularly from the left of the Labor Party and the Greens.[56]

Notwithstanding the political posturing from elements of the left and rearguard protectionist rhetoric from the

CPSU on the virtues and integrity of the public sector, the reality is that like all contemporary broadcasters around the world, the ABC acquires its more expensive and expansive content in large part from independent producers. Beyond a consideration of the public policy issues, it simply does not have the in-house creative capacity, the skills base or the funding, to do otherwise. However, it does so in the context of a market which suffers from the inherent structural problem that broadcasters have disproportionate negotiating strength compared with small independent producers. This issue is not confined to the ABC. It exists in Australia between commercial broadcasters and independent producers. It has also been an issue in the UK and in this case government intervention, and recognition of the sustainability of the independent sector as a public policy objective, have resulted in the emergence of the world's largest and most dynamic independent production sector.

The BBC

In the UK, local content, including higher-budget genres such as drama, documentary and children's programs, dominate broadcasting schedules, the result of a combination of a well-funded public broadcasting sector and a large domestic market. However, from the 1980s policy interventions have focused on structural and industry issues about how that content is produced. The new public publisher-broadcaster Channel 4 was set up in order to give 'producers the chance to make television programmes without the need to own or operate a broadcasting licence or be employed by a broadcaster'.[57] Soon after, independent production quotas were introduced for the BBC and, following that, regional production quotas. In a 2006 review the UK broadcasting regulator, Ofcom, re-stated the policy objectives for an independent production sector. Relevant to Australia and the ABC are: to promote cultural diversity, new energies and voices, creativity and new talent; and the growth of small-to medium-enterprises.[58]

However, an expression of these worthwhile objectives was not enough. The production sector was based on a 'fee-for-service', 'work for hire, 'costs plus' business model, and in the view of the sector—and ultimately the Government—the long-term development of its creative and commercial sustainability was constrained. Furthermore, small independent producers did not have the market power to deal with unfair pricing and a lack of rights ownership. To achieve the policy objectives around cultural diversity, creativity and enterprise development, government intervention around the business relationship between broadcasters, including the BBC, and independent producers was required.

The end result of a long and drawn-out political and policy process was a commitment in 2003 by the Blair Government Culture Secretary, Tessa Jowell, in which she recognised 'the essential role that the independent sector will have to play in the future of broadcasting in this country'.[59] The UK Government established a Code of Practice which included a requirement for broadcasters to negotiate with the independent production sector and enter into terms of trade that were fair and reasonable, including a transparent approach to setting licence fees, the ownership of rights and arms-length dealing on distribution agreements. The negotiation and implementation of the Terms of Trade agreement was to be overseen by the UK regulator, Ofcom.

What is important in the context of this paper is that this critical policy intervention was applied to the whole public broadcasting sector, including the BBC. The way the BBC and other broadcasters conducted their relationship with independent producers impacted the well-being and viability of the independent sector and in turn impacted national cultural and creative outcomes. According to Ofcom: 'A thriving independent sector has been credited with helping to bring new creative ideas to broadcasters and helping to stimulate creativity and quality'.[60] At no stage was there ever a suggestion that somehow the BBC's 'independence' was being threatened or impinged.

In Australia, the basis of broadcasting policy interventions related to Australian content have gone to issues of volume, diversity of genres and production costs. Various measures have been introduced and refined over the years including content quotas for the networks, expenditure commitments for pay television, and targeted or special funding from time to time for the public broadcasters. At times, funding to the public broadcasters has been aimed at content commissioned from the independent production sector. In addition, interventions have been made to deal with market failure in the financing of the content, including tax-based measures, which the commercial broadcasters are able to access, and direct funding through government agencies which is only accessible to independent producers.

In Australia interventions with regard to the commercial arrangements around how content is produced have been limited to measures taken by funding agencies, such as establishing minimum licence fees, in support of their brief to develop a local industry. In the UK, however, a leading creative industries consultant and strategic adviser has argued that the Codes of Practice and the agreed Terms of Trade established under the UK 2003 Communication Act are the most significant structural intervention in the UK's legislative and policy framework. They support an independent production sector and are what have made the UK independent sector a 'highly valuable and productive part of the UK's creative economy'.[61]

It is difficult to imagine any Australian government introducing a terms of trade regime across the whole of our broadcasting sector. Resistance from the commercial broadcasters and pay television operators would be too great. However, measures to ensure the ABC deals fairly with independent producers should form part of a broader strategy around ABC engagement with the independent production industry and creative sector. Such an arrangement could also serve to provide a best practice reference point for the broader industry.

6. An agenda for change

In concluding this paper I have outlined below measures which could form an agenda for change and which could transform the ABC's Australian content output and its relationship with the independent production sector. The ABC itself will resist any attempt to impose a framework of policy requirements and outcomes. And it will be supported in this opposition by a broad range of loyal and well-meaning supporters. The debate around the ABC for the most part is binary and sterile. One side claims that the ABC is simply underfunded and that any suggestion of imposing on it a set of expectations and outcomes is a threat to its independence. The other side focuses only on the news and current affairs output and claims that the ABC is politically biased and overfunded.

What I set out to establish in this paper is the profound disconnect between the ABC and its public policy settings concerning Australian screen content, and its contribution to Australian culture and identity. What we have seen consistently is that our most significant cultural institution is vulnerable to unilateral internal change, contrary to stated government policy and in the absence of any public discussion or review. The ABC's management and Managing Director, working to a politically appointed Board that lacks depth of experience—in broadcasting and screen content creation in particular and the arts and journalism more generally—is able autonomously to reset the priorities of the ABC.

To achieve its public responsibilities our most significant cultural organisation requires a governance structure within which its public purpose is clearly articulated and set by Government, where certain outcomes are clearly established and where the normal high standards of public sector accountability and transparency are mandated and adhered to. At present the ABC's self-proclaimed and all-encompassing independence causes it to exist in a state of isolation, untroubled by discussion and debate about its role within the Australian broadcasting and cultural sectors.

When the ABC was established in the 1930s Australia looked to the BBC as a model. When television was introduced in the 1950s once again Australia looked to the BBC for guidance. As we move into the digital era we could do worse than look again at how the UK Parliament over the years has resourced the BBC and has protected its independence; but also made a number of important policy-based interventions.

The Australian Parliament's statement of the ABC's public purpose is essentially its much revered Charter— less than four hundred words written more than a quarter of a century ago that comfortably fit within a single A4 page. In contrast, the UK Parliament reviews and renews the BBC's foundation document, its Royal Charter, every ten years.[62] This Charter sets out in considerable detail the BBC's Public Purposes including 'To show the most creative, highest quality and distinctive output' and to 'support the creative economy across the United

Kingdom.' However, it also reviews and renews what is described in the Charter as a Framework Agreement between the Minister for Culture, Media and Sport and the BBC.[63] This sixty plus page Agreement establishes the requirement for an open and transparent Public Interest Test if the BBC should contemplate any significant change to its services that may affect its Public Purposes. It also requires the BBC to establish performance measures and targets in relation to its Public Purposes and, further, it authorises Ofcom to independently establish performance measures and to collect information as required to assess the performance of the BBC. The Agreement also imposes requirements on the BBC in relation to original programs, regional production and independent production; and provides a very specific instruction to the BBC to 'develop and publish a film strategy'. As noted earlier, the UK Parliament has mandated an agreement between the BBC and UK independent producers designed to ensure fair terms of trade and to support the sustainability and growth of their sector. For all of this, the UK Parliament demands very high levels of transparency and accountability.

Elsewhere in the world—Canada, Ireland, South Korea—we also find governance and regulatory measures being applied to public broadcasters to deliver public policy outcomes in relation to both local content and and its creation.[64] The Australian Parliament could and should do the same.

Australia has developed over more than forty years a policy framework to ensure there is a diverse range of Australian-produced programs on our television. Furthermore, we have also developed a policy framework to ensure an independent production sector has the capacity to participate in the production of these programs. Our commercial television industries are large in economic terms and the impact of a local television production industry on our broader creative industries is significant.

And then there is the ABC: Australia's national public broadcaster. Its output of Australian content at times sets the benchmark in quality but its volume is inconsistent and unpredictable. In terms of governance structures and its own operations and culture, it stands outside the policy frameworks we have in place. And its track record in developing and maintaining a productive partnership with the independent production sector is for the most part poor.

An opportunity exists for our industry associations and guilds, and more generally supporters of the ABC, to jointly develop a coherent policy for the ABC and promote it to our political parties and Parliament. My proposed agenda is:

1. The Liberal Party, National Party and Labor Party develop comprehensive and long-term policy agendas for the ABC as part of their arts and cultural policies. These policies should:

    •   Commit to establishing governance measures that ensure the ABC broadcasts high levels of Australian screen content across all genres and in particular minimum levels of Australian drama, children's and documentary content.

- Acknowledge the importance of the relationship between the ABC and the independent production industry, propose the introduction of independent production quotas including regional quotas, and the development of an independently adjudicated terms-of-trade agreement between the ABC and Screen Producers Australia.

- Commit to mandating a high level of transparency and accountability in ABC reporting to Parliament.

2. The ABC's Charter be amended to include a commitment to Australian screen content and support for the growth and sustainability of Australia's screen production industry and creative sector.

3. A governance mechanism be developed through the Charter, in the form of a Ministerial Statement of Expectations or

an Agreement administered through the Government's independent regulator, the Australian Communications and Media Authority, that addresses:

- the ABC's volume and diversity of Australian content, in particular the genres of drama, documentary and children's programs.

- the ABC's engagement with, and support for, the growth and sustainability of Australia's production industry and creative sector.

- full and open transparency and accountability in ABC reporting

4. The ABC and Screen Producers Australia develop a Terms of Trade agreement, overseen by an independent referee such as Screen Australia, that supports the growth and sustainability of the independent production sector.

5. Eligibility for membership of at least half the ABC Board include some level of experience and understanding of the screen content creation sector.

The need for action

The changes we are seeing in our media landscape are profound and fast moving. However, in the area of screen content, these changes are largely about the business models that underpin the production and distribution of content and the technology that enables its consumption. The nature and the importance of the content itself remains largely unchanged. Long form, professionally produced, content continues to dominate our screens and what we watch.

When the medium of television arrived in Australia we developed a policy framework to ensure that our Australian stories, Australian faces and Australian voices were given some space. That framework has served us well and we have developed a vibrant commercially and creatively successful television industry that produces the most watched programs on our screens. However, that framework will increasingly be challenged by advancing digital technology changing how we receive and view our television content.

The ABC as a public broadcaster is in the privileged position of being able to engage actively and innovatively with the new digital landscape, free from commercial constraints. Its role as a provider of Australian stories and as a supporter of our local production sector can only grow in importance. But it has entered, and is operating in, this new landscape without the protection of any public policy framework to ensure a commitment to Australian content and the production sector that creates it. And it has already shown its disregard for this content, disdain for the production sector and disrespect for the adult and children's audiences that like to watch Australian programs.

The evidence before us clearly demonstrates some urgency for action and an agenda for change.

Postscript

As I conclude this paper, the ABC's managing director, Michelle Guthrie, has announced a plan to redirect funds from management and establish a 'content fund'. The immediate point to be made is that for an organisation whose core business should be content to feel the need to have a special 'content fund' speaks of a fundamental disconnect. Beyond this, and without wanting to sound churlish, this initiative is symptomatic of the fundamental concerns I have raised. It is another management plan conceived entirely within the institution and with no reference to the broader cultural and creative industry context in which the ABC operates. There is no detail or transparency about how it supports broader policy outcomes or indeed how its success or otherwise will be measured or reported. It does nothing to detract from the point that the ABC is operating outside of a broader public policy framework and that measures are required to correct this situation.

Endnotes

1. www.abc.net.au/news/2009-12-05/kevin-rudd-switches-on-abc3/1165184.
2. theconversation.com/no-dramas-what-budget-cuts-signal-for-homegrown-childrens-shows-on-abc3-50004.
3. 'ABC TV's Redfern Now launched under the stars', 1 November 2012, www.theaustralian.com.au/business/media/abc-tvs-redfern-now-launched-under-the-stars/news-story/df756296ebd848dff8f6eed0c7f21f79.
4. K.S. Inglis, *This is the ABC: the Australian Broadcasting Corporation 1932-1983* (Melbourne: Black Inc, 1983), p.193.
5. *Television, Make it Australian: a review of the need for Australian television content regulations*, Collingwood, Vic.: Television, Make it Australian, c. 1988, p.10.
6. *Television, Make it Australian,* p.12.
7. Inglis, *This is the ABC,* p.139.
8. Nick Herd, *Networking: commercial television in Australia* (Sydney: Currency House, 2012), p. 106.
9. Herd, *Networking,* p.110.
10. *Television, Make it Australian,* p.12.
11. *Television, Make it Australian,* p.13.
12. Herd, *Networking,* p.118.
13. Anti-siphoning refers to the regulatory arrangements in place to ensure that free-to-air broadcasters have the first right to a defined list of sporting events over and above pay television operators.
14. Herd, *Networking,* p.119.
15. *Television, Make it Australian,* p.35.
16. *Television, Make it Australian,* p.36.
17. David Throsby & Glenn Withers, *What Price Culture?,* North Sydney: Australia Council, 1984, pp.16, 26.
18. acma.gov.au/Industry/Broadcast/Television/Australian-content/australian-content-television.
19. K.S. Inglis, *Whose ABC?: the Australian Broadcasting Corporation 1983-2006* (Melbourne: Black Inc, 2006), p.328.
20. Inglis, *Whose ABC?,* p.347.
21. Inglis, *Whose ABC?,* p.542.
22. Inglis, *Whose ABC?,* p.379.
23. The role of the ABC in Australian culture, http://about.abc.net.au/speeches/the-role-of-the-abc-in-australian-culture/.
24. Ben Eltham, *When The Goalposts Move,* Platform Paper 48 (2016), pp.22–7.
25. Eltham, *When the Goalposts Move,* p. 25.
26. Inglis, *Whose ABC?,* p.7.
27. Inglis, *Whose ABC?,* p.7.
28. *Australian Broadcasting Corporation Act 1983,* Section 6 'Charter of the Corporation', (1) (a) (ii) and (1) (c).
29. Department of Communications, *ABC and SBS Efficiency Study: draft report,* April 2014, p.101, online at http://www.minister.communications.

gov.au/__data/assets/pdf_file/0003/63570/ABC_and_SBS_efficiency_
report_Redacted.pdf.

30. *Journals of the Senate* 52, 15 September 2011, p.1481.
31. *ABC Strategic Plan 2013-2016: A clear direction for the ABC*, p.2.
32. Department of Communications, ABC and SBS Efficiency Study April
    2014 Draft Report p.101 http://www.minister.communications.gov.
    au/__data/assets/pdf_file/0003/63570/ABC_and_SBS_efficiency_report_
    Redacted.pdf.
33. *ABC Annual Report 2015*, p.3.
34. *ABC Annual Report 2016*, p.42.
35. *ABC Annual Report 2005*, pp.13, 66.
36. Inglis, *Whose ABC?*, p.566.
37. Inglis, *Whose ABC?*, p.5.
38. Inglis, *Whose ABC?*, p.5.
39. Inglis, *Whose ABC?*, p.5.
40. *A New ABC Television Channel Just for Children: the Coalition Government
    Election 2007 Policy*, online at pandora.nla.gov.au/pan/22107/20071113-
    1021/www.liberal.org.au/about/documents/ABCChildrensChannel.pdf.
41. The FABC were quick to politicise the initiative and firmly position
    it within the prism of the ABC's independence. They described the
    announcement as 'a further abuse of the independence of the ABC' (www.
    abc.net.au/news/2007-11-10/plan-for-abc-kids-channel-draws-fire/721840)
    arguing that the ABC should not be told by government what services it
    should deliver or how it should spend its funds. Less than twelve months
    later with the Labor Party in power their position had changed. The
    proposal for a children's channel now had their support and it is described
    in their newsletter as a 'major issue [...] a popular issue [...] a motherhood
    issue.' (*Friends of the ABC Quarterly Newsletter* 10:2 (June 2008).
42. 'Australian Broadcasting Corporation — Australian content for ABC TV
    Expense ($m)', *Australian Government Budget Paper No 2, 2006-07*, online
    at www.budget.gov.au/2006-07/bp2/html/bp2_expense-03.htm.
43. Bob Mansfield, *The Challenge of a Better ABC*, Canberra: AGPS, 1997.
44. *Australian Labor Party, National Platform and Constitution, 2007*, pp. 277-
    82, online at parlinfo.aph.gov.au/parlInfo/search/display/display.w3p;quer
    y%3DId%3A%22library%2Fpartypol%2F1024541%22.
45. Stephen Conroy, Media Release 'Budget 2009: more Australian stories
    from ABC and SBS', 12 May 2007, online at pandora.nla.gov.au/
    pan/80090/20091110-0000/www.minister.dbcde.gov.au/media/media_
    releases/2009/035.html.
46. The Senate, Environment and Communications References Committee,
    Recent ABC programming decisions, October 2011, online from www.aph.
    gov.au/Parliamentary_Business/Committees/Senate/Environment_and_
    Communications/Completed_inquiries/2010-13/abc/hearings/index .
47. *Creative Australia: national cultural policy*, (Canberra: Commonwealth of
    Australia, 2013), online at apo.org.au/files/Resource/creative-australia_
    national_cultural_policy_0.pdf.
48. *Creative Australia*, p.32.
49. *Creative Australia*, p.46.
50. *Creative Australia*, p.83.
51. *Creative Australia*, p.46.
52. *ABC Annual Report 2008-2009*, p.85.
53. 'ABC funding to be cut by $254 million over five years, Communications
    Minister Malcolm Turnbull says', *Sydney Morning Herald*,
    20 November 2014 online at www.abc.net.au/news/2014-11-19/

abc-funding-cuts-announced-by-malcolm-turnbull/5902774.

54. In the NSW FABC's *Newsletter* 16:4 (September 2007) the then secretary of the ABC section of the CPSU, Graeme Thomson, is quoted as saying ABC TV's strategy of working with independent producers 'has turned the ABC into a broadcast transmission tower for other people's programs'. This was followed in the FABC *Background Briefing Quarterly Newsletter* 11:2 (July 2009) by 'ABC [TV] management [...] prefers to do business with the private sector' and it should 'stop this nonsense about calling it the "independent" sector'.

55. The FABC's *Background Briefing Quarterly Newsletter* 9:3 (September 2007) commenting on additional funding to the ABC for independently produced drama editorialised. 'the independence of the ABC is threatened by these moves. Australian culture will be the great loser'.

56. In their submission to the October 2011 Environment and Communications References Committee review *Recent ABC programming decisions* the Greens stated that 'commercial success and ratings and resale value on the part of [independent producers] skew decisions about content and [lead to a] homogenous "commercial" voice', and a few dot points later they stated that outsourced production lessens the ABC's ability to obtain 'revenue from resale and the licensing of products'. Online from www.aph.gov.au/Parliamentary_Business/Committees/Senate/Environment_and_Communications/Completed_inquiries/2010-13/abc/report/index.

57. Olsberg SPI, *Impact of the 2003 Communication Act on UK Indie Producers* (London: Olsberg, 2015), p.6, online at www.o-spi.co.uk/wp-content/uploads/2016/02/CMPA-Terms-of-Trade-Report-by-Olsberg-SPI-04-06-2015.pdf.

58. Ofcom, *Review of the operation of the Television Production Sector,* 2015, para. 1.4, online at www.ofcom.org.uk/__data/assets/pdf_file/0028/82684/tv_production_sector_review.pdf.

59. www.theguardian.com/media/2003/sep/19/bbc.broadcasting.

60. Ofcom, *Public Service Content in a Connected Society*, 2104, online at www.ofcom.org.uk/__data/assets/pdf_file/0019/42580/psbr-3.pdf.

61. Olsberg, *Impact*, p.28.

62. downloads.bbc.co.uk/bbctrust/assets/files/pdf/about/how_we_govern/2016/charter.pdf.

63. downloads.bbc.co.uk/bbctrust/assets/files/pdf/about/how_we_govern/2016/agreement.pdf.

64. S. Park et al., 'Domestic Content Policies in the Broadband Age: a four-country analysis, (Canberra: University of Canberra, 2015) online at www.canberra.edu.au/research/faculty-research-centres/nmrc/publications/documents/Domestic-Content-Policy-Report.pdf.

FORTHCOMING

PUTTING WORDS IN THEIR MOUTHS:
The Personal, Political and Practical Work of the Playwright

Andrew Bovell

Andrew Bovell has worked as a playwright and screen-writer for more than thirty years. In Platform Paper 52, he draws on this broad experience to discuss the place and role of the writer in the Australian theatre, film and television industries and examines how that place may have changed in each. He examines some of the philo-sophical, political and practical ideas that inform his work and makes a case for the centrality of the writer in the creative process whilst discussing the crucial relationship he has with other key creatives in the development of a new work.

AT YOUR LOCAL BOOKSHOP FROM 1 AUGUST
AND AS A PAPERBACK OR ONLINE FROM
OUR WEBSITE AT
WWW.CURRENCYHOUSE.ORG.AU

COPYRIGHT
INFORMATION

PLATFORM PAPERS
Quarterly essays from Currency House Inc.
Founding Editor: Dr John Golder
Editor: Katharine Brisbane
Currency House Inc. is a non-profit association and resource centre advocating
the role of the performing arts in public life by research, debate and publication.

Postal address: PO Box 2270, Strawberry Hills, NSW 2012, Australia
Email: info@currencyhouse.org.au Tel: (02) 9319 4953
Website: www.currencyhouse.org.au Fax: (02) 9319 3649

Editorial Committee: Katharine Brisbane AM, Michael Campbell, Dr Robin
Derricourt, Professor Julian Meyrick, Martin Portus, Dr Nick Shimmin, Greig
Tillotson

MISSING IN ACTION: The ABC and Australia's Screen Culture

ISBN 978-0-9946130-3-5
ISSN 1449-583X

Typeset in Garamond
Printed by McPherson's
Production by XOU Creative